Little Mitchie

ANTS THAT BUILD CITIES

TINY BUT MIGHTY!

TRACY VONDER BRINK

CREATING YOUNG NONFICTION READERS

Little Mitchie books spark curiosity and support early nonfiction reading for students in Grades 2-3. Designed to build vocabulary, support second language learners, and prepare readers for middle-grade content, each book includes helpful tips for parents and educators to build confidence and deepen understanding of the world.

TIPS FOR READING NONFICTION WITH BEGINNING READERS

Talk about Nonfiction

Begin by explaining that nonfiction books give us information that is true. The book will be organized around a specific topic or idea, and we may learn new facts through reading.

Look at the Parts

Most nonfiction books have helpful features. Our *Little Mitchie* titles include color photographs and graphic aids, a table of contents, a glossary, and an index. Share the purpose of these features with your reader.

Color Photos and Graphic Aids

A lot of information can be found by "reading" photos, charts, maps, and other graphic aids found within nonfiction texts. Help your reader learn more about the different ways information can be displayed.

Table of Contents

Located at the front of the book, this list shows the big ideas within the text and the page numbers where they can be found.

Glossary

Located at the back of the book, the glossary defines key words and phrases that are related to the topic. These words and phrases can be found in the text in colored type.

Index

Located at the back of the book, an index is an alphabetical list of topics and the page numbers where they can be found.

With a little help and guidance about reading nonfiction, you can feel good about introducing a young reader to the world of *Little Mitchie* nonfiction books.

Little Mitchie is an imprint of:

Mitchell Lane
PUBLISHERS

2001 SW 31st Avenue
Hallandale, FL 33009
mitchelllanepub.com

First Edition, 2027.

Author: Tracy Vonder Brink
Designer: Jen Bowers
Editor: Tricia Hoffman

Library of Congress Cataloging-in-Publication Data
Title: Ants That Build Cities / by Tracy Vonder Brink

Description: Hallandale, FL :
Mitchell Lane Publishers, [2027]

Identifiers:
ISBN 979-8-89260-884-8 (library bound)
ISBN 979-8-89260-987-6 (eBook)

Library of Congress Control Number: 2026936356

PHOTO CREDITS
Shutterstock: cover, p.1 ©2013 corlaffra, p.5 ©2020 Dr.MYM, p.5, 22 ©2020 JJ van Ginkel, p.6 ©2010 Eric Isselee, p.8, 22 ©2009 kurt_G, p.9 ©2020 Pascal Guay, p.11 ©2023 pryzmat, p.12–13 ©2018 Jackizms, p.15 ©2023 Aleksandrkozak, p.16–17, 22 ©2016 Pavel Krasensky, p.18 ©2020 Erik Agar, p.21 ©2016 Vyaseleva Elena

TABLE OF CONTENTS

Chapter One

BEING STRONG

Ant nests can be like underground cities. Most ants could fit on your fingertip. How do these tiny creatures build such big nests?

MIGHTY MOMENT
Ant nests have many tunnels and **chambers**. The tunnels are like roads, and the chambers are like rooms.

Ants are strong for their size. They can carry 10 to 50 times their body weight. That's like you lifting a couch by yourself! Ants use their strength to dig into hard ground and move soil.

An ant's **mandibles** snap shut with a **force** that's hundreds of times its body weight! These jaws are often covered in small, pointy tips that help ants get a good grip.

MIGHTY MOMENT

Ants use their mandibles to move soil, leaves, sticks, and small rocks as they make their nests. They also use their mandibles to catch food and fight enemies.

Chapter Two

BUILDING SMART

Ants are great builders. They know which pieces of soil are safe to dig out. They also know which to leave alone. Understanding which to move helps them dig tunnels that don't **collapse**.

MIGHTY MOMENT

How do ants know where and how to dig? Scientists have been trying to figure that out for years!

Ants usually dig straight down. A straight line is the shortest **distance** between two points. Digging a straight tunnel takes less work than one that curves back and forth.

Chapter Three

WORKING TOGETHER

Ants live in a **colony**. One colony can have millions of ants! They work together the same way you might play as part of a team.

MIGHTY MOMENT

There may be more than 15,000 different kinds of ants. They live everywhere except very cold places like Antarctica.

Ants have different jobs. The queen lays eggs, and some worker ants care for the young. Others look for food. Some ants are builders, while others protect the nest. They all help the colony.

Ants can't talk, but they **communicate**. Their bodies make special smells that other ants sense with their **antennae**. The smells mean things like, "Come this way for food," or "Fight this enemy!"

Chapter Four

AMAZING ANTS

Being strong, building smart, and working together helps ants make amazing nests. The world's largest ant colony stretches about as far as the distance across the United States. Tiny ants are some of the world's best builders!

MIGHTY MOMENT

Ant nests are not all the same. What they build depends on the kind of ant and where they live. Some nests are underground, but others are in trees. Some ants don't build nests at all!

A CLOSER LOOK

The queen ant is the largest in the colony. Some kinds of queen ants live more than 30 years.

Some ant nests only have one or two chambers. Large nests may have more than 100!

All ants have mandibles, but they're not all the same. Mandibles can be many different shapes and sizes.

GLOSSARY

antennae (an-ten-ee) feelers on the head of an insect

chambers (chaym-burz) rooms

collapse (kuh-laps) to fall down suddenly

colony (kah-luh-nee) a large group of animals that live together

communicate (kuh-myoo-ni-kate) to share information, ideas, or feelings

distance (dis-tuhns) the space between two places

force (fors) strength or power

mandibles (man-duh-buhls) the biting mouthparts of some insects

FURTHER READING

Bunting, Philip. *The Wonderful Wisdom of Ants.* Crown Books for Young Readers, 2024.

DK. *Ant Antics.* DK Children, 2023.

ON THE INTERNET

10 Cool Facts About Ants!

www.natgeokids.com/uk/discover/animals/insects/ant-facts/

National Geographic Kids shares their 10 favorite ant facts.

Ants

https://kids.britannica.com/kids/article/ant/352759

Learn about ants' size, their life cycle, and more with Britannica Kids.

INDEX